because
two are
better
than one,

for you, Daughter

Michelle

with love,

Mother

date

August 2, 2005

Our purpose at Howard Publishing is to:

- *Increase faith* in the hearts of growing Christians
- *Inspire holiness* in the lives of believers
- *Instill hope* in the hearts of struggling people everywhere

Because He's coming again!

You and Me, Daughter © 2004 by Chrys Howard
All rights reserved. Printed in Mexico
Published by Howard Publishing Co., Inc.
3117 North 7th Street, West Monroe, LA 71291-2227

04 05 06 07 08 09 10 11 12 13   10 9 8 7 6 5 4 3 2 1

Edited by Between the Lines
Interior design by LinDee Loveland and Stephanie D. Walker

ISBN: 1-58229-379-1

Scriptures not otherwise marked are taken from the HOLY BIBLE, NEW INTERNATIONAL VERSION ®. Copyright © 1973, 1978, 1984 by International Bible Society. Used by permission of Zondervan Publishing House. All rights reserved.

because two are better than one

you
and
me

Daughter

Chrys Howard

HOWARD
PUBLISHING CO.

Printed in Mexico

you

a

You taught me that
family can also be spelled
F-R-I-E-N-D!

Daughter

She discovered with great delight
that one does not love one's children
just because they are one's children
but because of the friendship
formed while raising them.

Gabriel Garcia Marquez

The Next Level

Climbing the waterfall hadn't looked that dangerous, but for Jane and her daughters the afternoon had suddenly taken a scary turn. An indescribable pain seared Jane's leg as her daughter Ashley struggled to free her. Jane was doing her best not to panic, but as each second passed she feared that her leg would break from the combined weight of the rushing water and Ashley's hands trying to pry her loose. Her older daughter, Korie, was carefully working her way to the side of the waterfall to get help.

The crisis started when the three women had enthusiastically joined a cruise to celebrate Jane's fiftieth birthday. While she loved her husband dearly, this was to be a trip of bonding with her daughters, now adults with children of their own—seven between them. It was a time in their lives when even stealing a lunch date was difficult. Being able to go away with her girls was the ultimate dream come true.

Jane was determined to defy the passing years and do everything her grown kids did. She wouldn't let the fact that she had gained a few pounds and was more than slightly out of shape keep her from enjoying this special trip. So far, things had been perfect. They had participated in the snorkeling tour the day before, ready for new adventures. The trio had explored coral reefs and pointed to brightly colored fish swimming beneath them. Stingrays had grazed their legs, and they giggled while trying to stand perfectly still in the midst of the entrancing sea creatures. It had been hard to smile with all the snorkeling equipment on, but Jane couldn't help it as she watched her daughters swim gracefully through the warm, clear water, tapping each other on the shoulder with each new discovery.

"Let's climb Dunn's River Falls when we get to Jamaica tomorrow," Ashley had said the night before as they were exploring their options for the next day. Ashley was the athlete of the family. In high school she had been the state triple-jump champion and had gone on to run track in college. Now twenty-five, married, and with three kids, she was still in great shape and always ready for a physical challenge.

But reading the brochure made Jane uneasy. Walking up a waterfall sounded crazy, even if it was a big Jamaican tourist attraction.

"Precaution should be taken at this activity," she read aloud to her daughters.

"Mom, you can do it," Korie had said confidently. "You were a swimmer in high school, an athlete. You'll probably do better than I will."

"Yeah, right," Jane had said to her twenty-nine-year-old as she continued to read. Secretly, she was hoping the brochure would declare an age limit and fifty would be too old. Jane didn't want to be a party pooper, but high school was a long time ago.

The whole week had been amazing, from their tastefully decorated cabin to the nightly midnight buffet. Jane wanted to do it all, but this climb might be beyond her limit.

Still, she was thrilled that her daughters had so much faith in her. She took a deep breath. "All right," she said. "I can do it! Let's go sign up." She would do her best to live up to the expectations of the two people who still believed she was invincible.

The morning started off uneventfully. The ship docked in Jamaica on time, and they were able to find transportation to the falls easily. Jane's stomach was a little uneasy. She wasn't sure if it was fear or the result of enjoying the midnight buffet more than she should have. She reached into her purse and found something to settle the rolling and then relaxed as the bus drove them through what looked like paradise.

"We have to rent these shoes," Ashley said as they disembarked at the falls. She led her mother and sister to a makeshift booth with handmade baskets filled with rubber shoes of all sizes. "These will keep us from slipping on the rocks," Ashley explained. "I read about them in the brochure."

Thirty dollars later, they were flopping toward the end of the water-fall in bright pink rubber shoes. Ashley and Korie laughed at the sight of their mother in her black one-piece bathing suit with the little skirt designed to make her look slimmer and the iridescent pink shoes.

Jane quickly came to appreciate what a wise investment the shoes were as she and the girls attempted to climb a cascade of water flowing over huge boulders. They had opted not to hire a guide to take them up the waterfall, but it didn't take a professional to make them realize the journey would be a challenge.

"It's so slippery!" Jane remarked through gritted teeth. "I'm thankful for these shoes."

Suddenly Jane came face to face with a huge hurdle—a three-foot step. "Oh, my!" she gasped, daunted as she watched Ashley scramble up the slippery rock.

"Mom, take my hand!" Ashley yelled down.

"You can't lift me up there," Jane protested. Her daughter's confidence in her own strength made her laugh.

"I'll push from behind," Korie yelled over the sound of rushing water.

Soon Jane was up on the rock with Ashley, catching her breath after the effort. Korie followed quickly behind. They took the opportunity to rest and assess the next level of their journey. Ashley decided they should stay to the right side of the falls. She had heard it was easier than the path on the left. Jane didn't argue but wistfully eyed an exit to solid ground for climbers who couldn't make it to the top.

No, I'm going to make it, she thought with determination. *The girls would be disappointed if I didn't.*

"Let's go," Korie said. "We have to be back at the bus by three o'clock, and we don't know how much longer it'll take to reach the top."

Looking ahead, Jane was relieved to see that the path looked easier for some distance. She confidently approached the thirty-foot flat stretch and started walking faster, ever conscious of the rocks that threatened to scrape her shins. Just as she was beginning to feel a little more secure, her left leg sank into water up to her knee, and her foot became wedged tightly in a crevice between two rocks.

"I'm stuck," Jane said, more calmly than she felt.

"Mom, are you serious?" Ashley said as she carefully made her way to her mother's side. "We're coming. Hold on!" Korie was right behind her.

For several minutes they all worked, trying to wedge a hand between the rock and Jane's calf to pry it loose.

"I'm going for help," Korie finally said.

"No, Korie," Jane protested. "Let's stay together. I don't want you out there by yourself. What if something should happen?"

"Something *has* happened, Mom," Korie said soberly and practically. "I have to go. We can't get you out. I'll be careful," she promised, then she was off.

At that moment, watching her daughters' efforts to help her, she felt a pain in her heart greater than the one she felt in her leg. She couldn't help but worry more about Korie's safety than her own as she watched her older child skim over slick rocks at a speed faster than she should. Ashley stayed by Jane's side, gently working on her leg and reassuring her that they would get her out.

Suddenly, Ashley's determination paid off. Jane's leg slipped free from the rock. The jolt threw Ashley back into the water, but she recovered quickly.

"She's out!" she yelled out to Korie. "Come on back!"

"Carefully," Jane cautioned. She surveyed the damage to her leg. From her ankle to her knee on both sides, there were angry-looking scrapes. She was badly bruised, but nothing seemed to be broken.

"Mom, let's get out at the next exit," Ashley urged. "We've climbed enough for one day."

"No, Ashley," Jane argued. "I started on a journey with the two of you, and I intend to go the distance, whatever it takes."

The rest of the climb was a little slower, but Jane was exhilarated when she and her daughters reached the top together.

"Mom, we're so proud of you," Korie said as Jane settled into her seat on the tour bus—relieved, tired, and happy in spite of her bruises.

Proud of you. Jane thought of all the times she had said those words to her daughters and how special it must have made them feel. Now that the girls were grown, she not only had two wonderful daughters who loved her and believed in her, but they were capable women with whom she could enjoy a rich friendship. She felt pretty special herself.

Ten Things My Daughter Does That Make Me Smile

1 Sings a silly song we sang when she was growing up

2 Calls me for advice on how long to cook rice

3 Takes me to lunch

4 Puts the dishes in the dishwasher without being asked

5 Believes I can do anything she can do

6 Teaches a Sunday-school class

7 Asks me to watch the grandkids at my house while she cleans hers

8 Wants to look through old photographs

9 Wants me to take pictures of her pregnant belly

10 Says to her own children something I said to her when she was a child

you....

for all the hugs and kisses—
especially the ones you gave me
in front of your friends.

My Daughter, My Friend

Never in my wildest dreams did I imagine I'd have the incredible relationship I do with you, my daughter. I was a teenager in the late sixties and early seventies. It was a time of turmoil, when teens across the nation were rebelling against authority, against their parents.

"Don't trust anyone over thirty" was the battle cry angry college protesters often chanted. Personally, I never knew what they were so angry about; but in some odd way, their protests influenced all of us as a society. Consequently, teens didn't have the relationship with their parents that they should have had.

But the world moved past that time. The protesters grew up and had children of their own. Their view of people over thirty drastically changed once they passed that threshold themselves. Not only did they want to be trusted, they valued a relationship with their kids.

And once again, the times were different. While I never would have worn my mother's clothes, you and I share two closets full of clothes. We even listen to the same music and enjoy the same movies. You are such a neat person! I have been blessed to share these years—and so much else—with you. You are truly my best friend, and I can't imagine life without you.

I've even forgiven you for wearing my jeans and using all my nail polish!

Two are better than one, because

they have a good return for their

work: If one falls down, his friend

can help him up. But pity the man

who falls and has no one to help

him up! . . . Though one may be

overpowered, two can defend

themselves.

—Ecclesiastes 4:9–10, 12

My faithful Daughter,

You have shown me that two are better than one because we always accomplish more together than apart. You inspire and encourage me without pushing. And when my days are hard, I know you'll be right behind me, ready to pick me up. You're the best friend I could ever have.

Your loving mother

you

From your first toothless smile to your shiny new braces, you taught me the importance of laughter.

Daughter

The best and most beautiful things
in the world cannot be seen
or even touched. They must be felt
with the heart.

Helen Keller

Popsicle Blessings

"What color do you want?" Kim asked Ally. Her strong-willed, red-headed daughter was three, and Kim was bribing her back to good humor and cooperation after the tonsillectomy. Ally hadn't wanted to go to the hospital, and now that the surgery was over, she didn't want to stay. She crossed her arms and set her puffy little face with the most determined, fierce look of displeasure Kim had ever seen and refused to eat or drink anything, even to soothe her painful throat. Not even ice cream could budge her.

In desperation, Kim had tried Popsicles and finally achieved success. The bright colors and refreshing taste brought Ally back around to the enchanting little girl with captivating blue eyes Kim adored.

She knew Ally would choose a red Popsicle—it was her favorite color. Kim used the Popsicle to teach Ally an important lesson there in the hospital.

"Going to the hospital isn't a fun thing," she reasoned with Ally as she slurped her third red Popsicle that day. "But it's for your own good. Your throat hurts a lot right now, but it'll get better soon. And then it won't bother you anymore."

Ally said nothing as her mother continued. "And this Popsicle reminds us that something good often comes from something bad." Ally looked at Kim quizzically. "You can have all the red Popsicles you want while you're in the hospital," she told the little girl, whose face lit up in a big smile—the first in two days. "You don't have to take a single orange or purple one—just the red ones you love."

◦

Kim awoke from the dream with a smile on her face. She was surprised for a moment to find that she was once again in the hospital, but this time she wasn't there for her daughter. The woozy feeling in her head and the pain in her side quickly reminded her that it was twenty-five years later, and this time she was the patient. She wrinkled her forehead as she tried to remember if she had even been in a hospital since Ally's tonsil surgery—no, not even when Jim had died. No wonder her dreams had taken her back to that sweet Popsicle time.

Now Ally was twenty-eight—and still strong-willed—but she had grown into a remarkable young woman who had recently put her stubborn nature to good use.

"Mom, you *have* to see a doctor," Ally insisted one day after they had been shopping together.

"Honey, I'll be fine," Kim had responded, but deep down she was concerned too. Although it was a touchy subject and concerned medical symptoms of a personal nature, confiding in Ally about personal matters seemed appropriate. *Confiding is one thing; taking her advice is another,* Kim had thought as she kissed her daughter good-bye and headed home. Kim looked in the rearview mirror to see her daughter shaking a finger at her. *Mom knows best,* she reassured herself. *Or do I?*

Kim could understand Ally's fear. When Ally's father, Jim, had died three years earlier of a sudden heart attack, they all wished they could have done something to prevent it. But there had been no symptoms: no pain in the arm, no tightness in the chest. He had simply dropped dead during a racquetball game, leaving her a widow at forty-eight. Kim had been devastated but refused to wallow in grief for the rest of her life. Mostly she was determined not to become a burden to her only daughter.

But Kim had to admit that Ally seemed to enjoy her mother's company and value her friendship. About a year after Jim's death, Kim began to realize that Ally was the one calling *her* for lunch dates and movie nights. They were two friends needing each other.

Ally hadn't yet found the man of her dreams. Maybe her strong will interfered with her romantic interests; maybe her standards were too high—or her goals. Maybe it just wasn't the right time. Ally had so many things she wanted to do and accomplish—she never seemed at a loss when it came to purpose and fulfillment. Whatever the reason, she didn't seem worried about it. She had a job she loved and a busy social life. And Kim wasn't going to complain. Ally's single status had given her lots of time to pursue a genuine friendship with her mother, and Kim felt blessed. Perhaps it had even helped save her life.

How could I have been so foolish? Kim thought now as she struggled to move just an inch to the left. The pain almost brought her to tears, but she bit her lip and pushed the button for the nurse to bring her more pain medicine. Shaking her head, she realized the six-inch incision on her right side would forever remind her of her own stubbornness. *Now I know what scars are good for,* she thought. *To remind us that something bad happened, but we survived it.*

After that fateful shopping trip, Ally had taken it on herself to call a family friend who was a doctor.

She later confessed that she had told Dr. Bailey about her mom's nagging stomach pain and the unusual bleeding.

Dr. Bailey firmly emphasized that Kim needed to see a doctor soon.

"Mom, you have an appointment for a colonoscopy Friday morning," Ally had announced. "I'll drop by this afternoon with the doctor's instructions on how you need to prepare for it. And I'll be there at six sharp Friday morning to pick you up."

"Ally, no," Kim had protested.

"I won't take no for an answer," Ally said firmly. "Losing one parent is bad enough. I won't lose two!"

Ally did as she promised and came for her mother promptly at six. The weather was warm and muggy and seemed to overwhelm them even after they were in the car. Neither woman felt the need to talk. Their love for each other and their friendship didn't always require words.

The nurses and doctors had been fantastic. They kept Ally informed of her mother's progress every step of the way. Kim and Ally even managed to laugh as Kim was recovering from the anesthetic and kept asking nonsensical questions.

But the tone got serious very quickly as the doctor entered the room.

"You have a questionable scope," the doctor had said matter-of-factly, as though he were merely giving a weather report. Kim would never forget the look of fear in Ally's eyes as she reached over and grabbed her mother's hand.

"We need to wait for the pathology report to know for certain," the doctor continued. "I'll call as soon as I know something. Go ahead and get dressed. You may leave as soon as you feel steady enough."

Ally found her mother's clothes and lovingly helped Kim dress. Kim wasn't sure if it was the medication or the bad news that was making her feel a little shaky.

"It'll be all right," Ally kept reassuring her mother. "I just know it will be."

"I believe we caught it in the early stages," the doctor said the next day. While Kim would rather have heard there was no cancer, at that moment "early stages" sounded pretty good.

"You need to see an oncologist," Dr. Martin continued, "but I'd guess you're facing six weeks of chemotherapy, six weeks of rest, and then surgery to remove the remaining tumor.

"You can be very thankful you came in when you did," he told her. "Someone was looking out for you."

Kim had squeezed Ally's hand tightly. She fought back tears, not wanting Ally to see her cry. "She sure was," she said.

Kim hung up the phone and told Ally everything the doctor had said. Ally flew into action, making doctor appointments and searching the Internet for medical information. Kim had been awed by her daughter's professional manner when dealing with doctors and her sense of humor and strength when dealing with Kim.

Kim tried again to prop herself up in the hospital bed. Her back was aching from staying in one position so long, and the nurses had warned her to move around to prevent pneumonia. She wanted Ally to be there to help her, but she knew Ally couldn't always be there for her.

She closed her eyes and with a firm spirit prayed, "Thank You, God, for giving me a stubborn daughter. You knew twenty-eight years ago what I needed, and You provided Ally. Now, please help me get up on one elbow."

When she opened her eyes, there stood a smiling Ally. Dressed in jogging clothes with her red hair pulled up in a ponytail, she grinned impishly, her hands behind her back.

"What color do you want?" she asked her mother brightly.

"What?" Kim asked, confused. Then a smile brightened her face as she remembered—the blessing in the bad—her strong-willed Popsicle daughter.

"Oh yeah," she responded enthusiastically. "Red!"

Ten Things I Love
about My Daughter

1 Her steadfast devotion to her family—even her little brother

2 Her desire to be the best she can be

3 Her endless love for brushing my hair

4 Her dimples

5 Her patience when I give unsolicited advice

6 Her sweet tone even when she doesn't like the dress I picked out

7 Her optimism and faith that human beings, on the whole, sincerely want to do right

8 Her faithfulness to God and her desire to let her light shine

9 Her respect for me as her mother and her love for me as a friend

10 Her enthusiasm for new projects and her dedication to completing them

thank

you...

for being the kind of daughter others wish they had.

Tribute

A TRIBUTE TO MY DAUGHTER

My Daughter, My Joy

Even though you were the youngest in our family, you were the leader. Yes, we called you bossy when you were three and ordering everyone around, but as you got older, you learned to use your iron will and strong ideas positively. You became a leader in our family, at school, and with our church youth group. Your teachers would tell me they hated for you to miss school because you made the day so much fun for the other students.

How I loved seeing you interact with your peers. Their faces would light up, just as mine would when you entered a room. It has been an incredible blessing to have a daughter like you. I was a shy child, so having a child who is the complete opposite of me is fun. Just last year, on a cruise, you entered a Hula-Hoop contest and were crowned "Hula-Hoop Queen." The whole ship cheered as you spun your Hula-Hoop in front of a thousand people and then blew kisses as they crowned you queen. I could never do anything like that, but I sure enjoyed watching you!

You make every activity an adventure, and you inspire me to look for the joy in each day. You make me realize it's fun to laugh at yourself and to do things you're a little uncomfortable doing. I look forward to many years of love and laughter with you, my precious daughter!

Greater love has no one than this,

that he lay down his life for his

friends.

—John 15:13

My darling Daughter,

I know that in your lifetime pain will come to you. It grieves me, but it's true. I would lay down my life for you—take any illness, any financial burden, any heartache I could away from you. I know things don't often work out that way. But I want you to know, I'm willing.

Your devoted mom

I Remember

Laughing as I watched you swing,

Listening to you loudly sing.

Reading in our comfy chair,

Combing tangles from your hair.

Watching as you played a game,

Cheering when they called your name.

Hugging when you cried with fright,

Praying it would be all right.

Smiling as I watched you play,

Thanking God for every day.

you
a

Enjoying life with a
daughter like you makes
growing older easy.

God makes the world
all over again
when a child is born.

Jean Paul Richter

Expecting Love

"What was she like?" Kristy asked her father one more time in the labor room. The contractions were now four minutes apart, but even in the middle of labor, her desire to know her mother—just a little bit better—mingled with her desire to know her coming daughter.

"Kristy," her dad began with tears filling his eyes, "your mother would be so proud of you. You remind me of her on the night *you* were born. You know we prayed for you. Every night your mother rubbed her tummy and prayed, 'Please keep our baby safe and healthy . . . and, if you don't mind, we'd like a daughter!' Oh, Kristy, she'd be a wonderful grandmother. Just pretend she's here, holding your hand and coaching you through."

"Sir," a hurried nurse interrupted. "Could you step out? The doctor is ready to come in."

56

"Sure," Kristy's dad said as he squeezed her hand one more time. "It won't be long now, and your baby girl will be here."

Kristy closed her eyes as her father kissed her forehead. Another pain was coming, and while she welcomed it, knowing each pain brought her daughter closer to home, she was ready for some relief.

Kristy's husband, Justin, reached for her hand. She closed her eyes and kissed his hand but envisioned kissing baby Macy on her forehead just as her daddy had kissed her. She could almost feel the softness of her skin.

"Are you ready for something to stop that pain?" Dr. Green asked.

"Yes!" Justin said eagerly. "I'll answer for her." They had been in the labor room for five hours, and he was ready for some relief even if Kristy wasn't.

"I guess," Kristy said. "But you have to understand—I've waited a long time for this pain."

Dr. Green laughed. "I've never had a baby, and most mothers tell me they do forget the pain when it's over; but I still think you moms are pretty brave. I'll get your epidural ready, and soon you can stop focusing on the pain and start focusing on your new daughter."

If he only knew, Kristy thought. *That's all I've focused on for years.*

❧

From the time Kristy could understand that she didn't have a mother, she wanted to know everything about her. "What was she like?" was the most-asked question in the Howell household.

"Well, Kristy," her dad would answer, "she was beautiful. She had a smile like a toothpaste commercial; but more importantly, she loved you so very much and wanted you more than anything. She would hold you and just stare at you for hours. Sometimes I would wake up in the middle of the night, and she wasn't in bed because she had fallen asleep holding you in the rocking chair." He always smiled as if he could still see it all. "I wish you could have seen her face when she got you out of bed each morning. It was as though she were seeing you for the first time."

As a child, Kristy's eyes would light up when her dad said that part. But as she got older it made her sad that she had no memory of her mother's touch or the sound of her voice. Try as she might, she couldn't remember a single one of the many kisses her dad promised had been lavished on her. She had pictures to remind her of what her mother looked like, but she desperately missed experiencing her personally.

Kristy had been only two when her mother was diagnosed with ovarian cancer. It was a fast-growing tumor, and she had only been given a year to live. The doctors did everything they knew to do, but one year and two months later, Kristy's mother died.

Kristy shifted her thoughts from the past to the present—and the future.

I know this pain will go away, she thought as she braced herself for another contraction, *but I'll have Macy forever. Forever—I love that word! Not only will I see Macy's first steps, but I'll see her walk down the aisle. I'll run beside her as she learns to ride a bike. I'll argue with her about wearing too much makeup, and I'll take her and a carload of friends to ball games. Macy, I hope you're ready for a mother who loves you as much as I do!*

Suddenly a stab of fear pierced her heart. Was this what her mother had felt when she had been born? Full of love, hopes, and dreams for her new little daughter, thrilled with the promise of someone she'd love forever? Only Kristy's mother hadn't had forever, and so many things had been left undone and unsaid. What if Kristy didn't have forever with her little daughter either? How could she bear to miss out on the milestones and everyday events that make up life and bind a mother and daughter together? The thought was almost more than Kristy could bear—far worse than the pain of childbirth that racked her body.

Then Kristy realized something that was oddly comforting: The pain and fear she felt at the prospect of her own loss was dwarfed by the emotions she felt for her daughter. Her heart was filled with love, pain, and a fierce protectiveness for the little girl yet unborn. She wanted to be there for this child—to provide everything she wanted and needed. She wanted Macy to know a mother's love—to feel her touch, to smell her perfume, to experience her kisses.

So this was what it felt like to be a mother—to love and feel a child's pain more acutely than your own, to care for her more than you care for yourself. Suddenly Kristy had a new understanding of the sorrow her mother must have felt knowing she would have to say good-bye. It made her appreciate and love her mother even more than she had before. Kristy wept.

I will do everything I possibly can to be there for you, Macy. Kristy's heart took the promise to her tiny daughter. *Whatever you need or want, I hope to be the person you can count on.*

"Are you OK?" Justin asked when he saw Kristy crying. "Is the pain too much?"

"It hurts, but I'm not crying because of the pain," Kristy told him. "I was just thinking about our daughter—and my mom. I think I understand everything a little better now."

Justin leaned over to kiss his wife. "I'm glad," he whispered tenderly. "I can't wait to see our daughter."

"Hi, honey," Kristy's father said as he opened the door to the delivery room. "The doctor said I could come in for one more hug."

"Oh, Daddy, can you believe it? I'm going to have a daughter today! In just a few minutes! I know I've told you before, but I have to say it again. Thank you for being both Mom and Dad to me. I know there were times when I wasn't so nice to be around—when I wanted a mom instead of a dad. But we made it, didn't we? Thank you for answering every question I had about Mom and for keeping her alive in my heart. I think I'm finally starting to understand what it's like to have a daughter—the hopes, the dreams, the fears, and the pain. I don't know how you managed it alone."

"Kristy, I love you so much," her dad responded. "When your mother died, we both missed out on a lot. So many times I wished it was her painting your nails or teaching you to jump rope. Not because I didn't want to do those things, but because she would have loved them so much. When Macy is born, I'm going to get to see your mother through you. And I can't wait."

"Dad, I know it was always you and me—just the two of us—and I wouldn't have traded that for anything, but Justin and our daughter are expanding that circle. I already love my little girl more than I ever imagined possible. Are you OK with that?"

"Kristy," her dad said smiling proudly, "I wouldn't have it any other way."

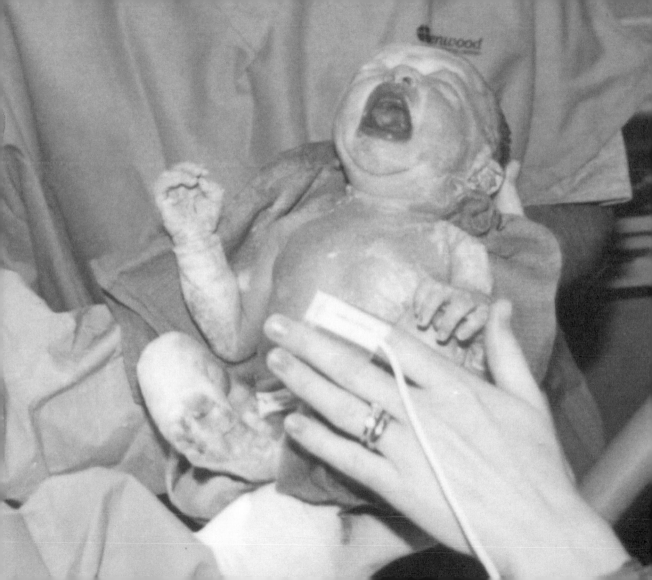

Ten Fun Things My Daughter and I Do Together

1 *Look for seashells*

2 *Shop*

3 *Teach classes*

4 *Talk on the phone*

5 *Plan parties*

6

Eat out

7

Go to the movies

8

Make Christmas cookies

9

Get pedicures

10

Work out

you...

*for coming into my bedroom at
night and asking for my advice.*

My Daughter, My Reassurance

When you told me you were pregnant, I had such mixed emotions. Part of me was eager and ready to see our future family. The other part felt I was too young to be a grandmother, and you were too young to be a mother. It seemed you had just walked down the aisle, and now you were announcing your first pregnancy. I wasn't so sure I was ready!

But pregnancy is a little like hide-and-seek, when the person doing the seeking calls out, "Ready or not, here I come!" Ready or not, I was about to become a grandmother, and you a mother.

I think I was more apprehensive than you were. But you—always sensitive and sweet—understood how much I needed to be a part of your pregnancy. You allowed me to share in doctor appointments and ultrasounds. The science of bringing babies into the world had changed in the twenty years since I delivered you, but you still lovingly asked my advice and listened as I lectured you about taking vitamins and getting enough rest.

Together we shopped for clothes and sewed baby curtains. We took pictures of your growing tummy and compared them with pictures of me when I was pregnant with you. Thank you, my sweet daughter, for sharing your children—your life—with me. Thank you for making me feel needed and important.

I always thank God for you

because of his grace given you in

Christ Jesus. For in him you have

been enriched in every way—

in all your speaking and in all

your knowledge. . . . He will keep

you strong to the end.

—1 Corinthians 1: 4–5, 8

Dear Daughter,

In the stillness of each night and in the quietness of early morning, I thank God for you. I can't imagine starting or ending my day without letting the Creator know that I'm thankful He created you. I know God has blessed you in many ways and will be there to keep you strong. You are my greatest treasure!

Your proud mom

you a

Your adventurous spirit challenges and inspires me to step out of my comfort zone and try new things.

Daughter

Give a little love
to a child, and
you get a great deal back.

John Ruskin

Pomp and Circumstance

The back of the gymnasium was a sea of black and white. Four hundred and fifty-three graduates, ready and eager to conquer the world, were waiting for the processional music to start the ceremony that would mark them as college graduates.

"Mom, what does it look like in there? Describe it to me," Brittany asked her mom, who was straining to see inside Brown Gymnasium where the spectators were gathering.

"Oh, Brittany, it's amazing," Sheila said, standing on her toes to see over the other graduates. She scanned the room for details to share.

"There's a stage at the front of the gym where all the important people will sit. The vice president's wife is dressed in a very proper light blue suit and is standing next to Dr. Baumgartner at the head of the line. Let's see, what else? Off to the side are the chairs for the professors. There's Dr. Matthews. Remember him from freshman English?" Sheila and Brittany both smiled at the memory. "Oh, Brittany, there must be six thousand people in there! People are everywhere, waving to family members, taking pictures."

Sheila looked down at her daughter. She looked just like any other college student, wearing Ray-Ban sunglasses and looking cool. But Brittany's sunglasses did more than block the sun or make her look cool. Brittany was blind.

Sheila's mind went back to Brittany's early years. As a baby and then a toddler, she developed like any other child. In many ways, she was ahead of other children. She was wiry and quick and had started walking at just nine months of age. By eighteen months she was speaking in complete sentences. Sheila and her husband, Robert, were convinced they had the perfect child.

"Robert, look at her," Sheila said one day as they played in the yard with Brittany. "Not only is she brilliant, she's going to be an athlete too!" Sheila was sure she was only exaggerating a little. At two and a half, Brittany could catch a ball if it was thrown right to her, and she could turn a somersault. "She has it all. Who would have thought we could produce such a promising child?"

"Certainly not our families," Robert responded with a smile.

Neither of their families had held much hope that Robert and Sheila would be able to succeed at much of anything. They had started dating when they were both just sixteen, and by seventeen, Sheila was pregnant with Brittany. Well-meaning family members had begged them to put the baby up for adoption. They had been convinced that the young couple couldn't possibly make it with a baby and no college education.

But Sheila and Robert had proven them all wrong. He went to work in his dad's carpentry shop and discovered he'd inherited his father's ability to build fine cabinets for expensive homes. Within five years, young Robert was in high demand for his talents.

Sheila finished high school and gave birth to Brittany two months later. Her life became wrapped up in caring for the baby. There was no time or money for college. Then tragedy struck.

"Robert," Sheila said one evening as they were clearing the dinner table. "Today I noticed something odd."

"What's that?" he asked.

"Brittany was looking at a book and was holding it about three inches from her face," Sheila answered. "Do you think she can see?"

"Oh, Sheila, don't jump to conclusions." Robert tried to calm her fears. "Brittany's only three. Maybe all three-year-olds look at books like that. Let's just watch her and see."

After a few weeks, Robert had to admit something was strange, and they took Brittany to an eye doctor.

"This isn't going to be easy for me to tell you," Dr. Matthews began. "Brittany has a rare disease. We have no cure, and she won't get any better. It starts out with a gradual loss of vision, as she's experiencing now, but eventually she'll lose her sight completely."

Sheila felt as though someone had knocked the air out of her. Her head was spinning, and she felt sick.

"Where else can we take her?" was Robert's first response. "Surely there are better hospitals, specialists. Someone can fix my little girl's eyes."

With great patience and a tender voice, Dr. Matthews replied, "No, I'm sorry, there isn't. I can refer you to other doctors, but they'll all tell you the same thing. This disease is degenerative. No one can make it better. But Brittany's young; she'll adjust. I can give you some names of people who have been through this with their children."

"I don't want a list of blind people," Sheila said softly, with tears streaming down her cheeks. "I just want Brittany to be OK."

In that one instant, all their dreams about Brittany had been dashed.

But they developed new dreams, and Brittany became an independent, well-adjusted young woman.

"Mom, go with me," Brittany begged one night during the spring semester of her senior year in high school. "You've always wanted to earn your degree. Now you can get one and help me get mine."

"Oh, Brittany, I'm too old to go to college. I'm not sure my brain will even work anymore." Sheila sighed as she looked through the stack of college-entrance materials the guidance counselor had sent home with Brittany.

Sometime during Brittany's sixth-grade year, when she had Mr. Corbett for history, she had announced that she wanted to be a teacher. Brittany's teachers had always been great and helpful, but Mr. Corbett was special. He had a way of showing history, not just telling it. His imagination awakened Brittany's as he described scenery she would never see, great battles led by dignified generals, and historic presidential elections.

"I want to do that," Brittany had told her mom. "I want to make history come alive for students."

"We'll do everything we can to make that happen for you," Sheila had promised. She hadn't thought it would mean going to college with Brittany, but Brittany was insistent.

"Mom, you know how much you wanted to go to college," she coaxed. "And don't say you're too old. Everyone asks me if you're my sister! We're just seventeen years apart. If I can do it, you can too. Come on. Think about it. We can help each other."

Sheila decided to mention it only casually to Robert, fearing he would think she was being silly.

"Robert," she began, "Brittany wants me to go to college with her."

"Now, Sheila," Robert said as he read the newspaper and flipped through the sports channels on TV. "You know we've always encouraged Brittany to be independent of us. Even though the college is right here in town, she still needs to do this alone. You don't need to go carry her books or drive her around campus."

"She doesn't want me there for that purpose, Robert. She wants me to go to college too. She wants me to take classes and get my own degree."

Robert put down the paper and turned off the TV. "Is that what you want to do?" Robert asked seriously.

"Well, I'm not sure," Sheila answered hesitantly. "My motherly duties are getting lighter, and as Brittany reminded me, I'm still pretty young. Of course I'm scared, but Brittany will be there with me. She says I can help her, but you know what? I'm going to be the one who will need help. I don't think I would have the courage to even think about going back to school without her encouragement."

Robert smiled. "She's pretty special, isn't she?" he said proudly. "And independent. You've given your life to make sure she could succeed on her own. Now she's ready to help you with some of your dreams. I guess I'll have two kids in college," he mused good-naturedly. "How about that?"

⌒

The music started, and the crowd came to their feet as the eager graduates walked down the center aisle of the gym single file—except Sheila and Brittany. The mother-daughter team walked together, arm in arm. Sheila caught a glimpse of Robert watching proudly from an aisle seat, not even bothering to hold back his tears of pride. And just like it had been during their four years in college, Sheila wasn't sure whether she was guiding Brittany or Brittany was holding her up. Maybe it was both. It didn't matter. They were there for each other. She gave Brittany's arm a special squeeze. Sheila couldn't have been happier or prouder to have her for a daughter.

Ten Lessons I've Learned from My Daughter

1 You're never too old to roller-skate.

2 One bedtime hug is capable of turning an OK day into a great one.

3 Pizza makes great breakfast food.

4 If you want to be good at something, you have to practice.

5 Children can give great advice.

6 *It's important to have a friend to confide in.*

7 *Some work can wait until tomorrow— so chill!*

8 *Forgiveness is easier than adults think.*

9 *If you aren't happy with the way you look, change it.*

10 *The nail color on your fingers doesn't have to match the color on your toes.*

you...

for the many times you said,
"You can do it, Mom!"

My Daughter, My Inspiration

There are so many things I do because you've inspired me to do them. Something tells me you would say the opposite is true—that I inspired you. But being the mother, I felt I was just doing my job. It wasn't your job, yet you inspired me every day.

Every time I watched you play a ball game, it inspired me to stay in shape so I could play too. Every time you brought home a good grade on an assignment, it inspired me to challenge my mind and to read more so I could have interesting conversations with you. Every time you wanted to have friends over, it inspired me to open my home to church members and friends from town so you would learn the gift of hospitality. Every time I saw you cry about the injustice in the world, it inspired me to reach out to a world different from my own through mission trips and summer camps.

It has been said that the best example is someone who walks the walk, not just talks the talk. You inspired me to go beyond talking to walking. One definition of inspiration is to convey something to another's heart and mind through extraordinary influence. I'd have to say that a mother-daughter relationship is just such an influence! You are an extraordinary daughter, and you've changed my life for the better.

Love is patient, love is kind. . . .

It always protects, always trusts,

always hopes, always perseveres.

—1 Corinthians 13:4, 7

My precious Daughter,

   Thank you for your patience and kindness when I'm not the mother I should be. That is truly love. Love also involves protection, trust, and perseverance—and I promise to do my best at all three in my relationship with you. I love you, and I'll always want the best for you.

                                        Mom

Dear heavenly Father,

Thank You for the precious gift You have given me in my daughter. From the moment I saw her, I knew You had formed and shaped her just for me. She has brought such joy to my life and taught me so much about the true meaning of unconditional love. Help me never to take this gift for granted and always to treat her with kindness and gentleness.

God, bless this sweet child of mine. Shower Your rich blessings upon her and wrap Your arms around her for safety. While I will not always be right beside her, You will. May she never lose sight of You, Lord, as she goes about each day.

Thank You, dear Lord, for creating this special relationship between my daughter and me.

Amen